GW01111083

Ripon

in old picture postcards

by
Ripon Civic Society

European Library - Zaltbommel/Netherlands MCMLXXXV

Compiled by Ripon Civic Society
Chairman: J.M. Younge MA
Editor: M.H. Taylor MA
Contributors: Mrs. E. Elis, Dr. W. Forster, Rev. A.W. Shepherd, Mr. A. Stride and Mr. J. Yarker

GB   ISBN 90 288 3323 4 / CIP

©1985 European Library - Zaltbommel/Netherlands

European Library in Zaltbommel/Netherlands publishes among other things the following series:

IN OLD PICTURE POSTCARDS *is a series of books which sets out to show what a particular place looked like and what life was like in Victorian and Edwardian times. A book about virtually every town in the United Kingdom is to be published in this series. By the end of this year about 175 different volumes will have appeared. 1,250 books have already been published devoted to the Netherlands with the title* **In oude ansichten.** *In Germany, Austria and Switzerland 500, 60 and 15 books have been published as* **In alten Ansichten;** *in France by the name* **En cartes postales anciennes** *and in Belgium as* **En cartes postales anciennes** *and/or* **In oude prentkaarten** *150 respectively 400 volumes have been published.*

For further particulars about published or forthcoming books, apply to your bookseller or direct to the publisher.

This edition has been printed and bound by Grafisch Bedrijf De Steigerpoort in Zaltbommel/Netherlands.

INTRODUCTION

The city of Ripon lies on the western edge of the Vale of York, at the foot of Wensleydale, close to the confluence of the Ure and the Skell.

Ripon owes its origin to Anglo-Saxon settlers, who had established a farming community between the two rivers by the 7th century. About the year 660 the King of Northumbria added a monastery, briefly to house the celebrated St. Cuthbert. A little later it passed to the tempestuous churchman Wilfrid, who also held Hexham abbey and the bishopric of Northumbria. From his considerable wealth he built in Ripon one of the finest churches of his day (672), and his memory has been revered in the city ever since.

The 300 years that followed his death in 709 were very disturbed, as Anglo-Saxon rulers fought among themselves as well as with the new Viking invaders. During those violent times Wilfrid's monastery in Ripon was destroyed (948) and his bones moved to Canterbury for safe keeping.

Norman Archbishops of York later rebuilt the church, now served by canons rather than monks, and in the 12th century dramatically changed the shape of Ripon itself. A new Norman borough was laid out, well to the west of the original Saxon settlement, and this purpose-built commercial centre soon provided the Archbishop with a considerable income from rents and tolls. The streets that radiated from the new Market Place also gave Ripon the same basic plan which it has today.

The new town flourished for the rest of the Middle Ages, despite Scottish raids. Cloth-making grew into a major industry, and pilgrims flocked to the shrine of St. Wilfrid in the great Minster Church. During those centuries the Norman Church was progressively enlarged and rebuilt, so that it broadly came to assume its present appearance, apart from the now absent spires. Unfortunately little else of mediaeval Ripon survives — part of North Bridge perhaps, and the chapels of two former hospitals or almshouses.

The Wars of the Roses largely passed Ripon by, but there was to be no escape from turmoil under the early Tudors. The cloth industry declined, Fountains Abbey was closed, the shrine of St. Wilfrid demolished, and the Catholic Mass ousted by the Protestant Communion Service. Those who resisted change were ruthlessly crushed — hundreds of rebels were executed in Ripon in 1570 after the unsuccessful Rising of the North.

More fortunate times followed under the Stuart King, James I. The lands filched from the Minster Church during the Reformation were partly restored, and the office of Dean created to head the Chapter of Canons. That same year, 1604, another royal charter also reorganised the government of the city. Whilst both Ripon and a large area around it (the Liberty of Ripon) had long been held by the Archbishops of York, responsibility for keeping law and order in the town rested with an official known as the Wakeman, who organised constables to patrol the streets, and set the night-watch by having a horn blown each evening at 9 pm in the Market Square — an ancient tradition that Ripon still maintains today. The charter of 1604 replaced the office of Wakeman with that of Mayor; the last Wakeman, Hugh Ripley, became the first

Mayor, and his house still stands in a corner of the Square.

A few years later, in 1617, James I was gratefully received on a brief visit and presented with a set of silver spurs at a time when Ripon spurriers had a national reputation. Some years later, both Charles I and Cromwell passed through the town in less happy times. From the close of the 17th century, Ripon came strongly under the control of the Aislabie family of nearby Studley Royal. John Aislabie, who landscaped the grounds there after the South Sea Bubble scandal abruptly terminated his parliamentary career (1720), was a good friend to Ripon and had earlier contributed generously to the cost of the new Obelisk in the Square, doubtless his inspiration. His son, William, was to represent Ripon in Parliament for sixty years.

During the 18th century local communications improved as the main approach roads were turnpiked and a canal built. By George IV's reign regular stage-coach services were operating from the Unicorn and Black Bull inns, providing rapid travel to Newcastle, Leeds and even London. Horse and cattle fairs were a great Ripon attraction in those days, but genteel society flourished too — a theatre was opened, an Assembly Room built, and new town houses constructed for the gentry.

In 1836 the Minster Church became a Cathedral with the establishment of the diocese of Ripon, and an imposing Bishop's Palace soon appeared on the outskirts of the city. In an age of rising population, however, the overcrowded tenement courtyards off the main streets suffered acute public health problems, and many people died in outbreaks of cholera, typhoid and dysentery.

On the brighter side, the Victorian Age also brought many improvements. In 1848 the railway came, soon to be followed by a new hospital and a new Workhouse. Education flourished: the ancient Grammar School moved to a more spacious setting on the edge of the town and a Training College opened for women teachers. New churches and new chapels mushroomed as Victorian religious fervour reached its height.

In Edwardian times Ripon tried briefly to emulate nearby Harrogate as a popular spa centre, despite the problem of having to pipe in the medicinal waters from several miles away. With the outbreak of war in 1914, however, visitors of a very different kind appeared — Belgian refugees and soldiers by the thousand, as a vast army camp was constructed. The Second World War again brought servicemen to Ripon, this time often RAF personnel from airfields in the Vale of York. Today the Royal Engineers base maintains the service connection as strongly as ever. Since 1945 Ripon has grown considerably in size, modernising its schools and housing, developing new light industries, and attracting ever-growing numbers of tourists. Local Government reorganisation in 1974 transferred the work of the former City Council to Harrogate, but Ripon still proudly maintains its status of city, recently confirmed by special royal charter.

J.M. Younge

1. The focal point of the Market Place is the obelisk, built in 1702 by John Aislabie of Studley Royal, then Mayor of Ripon. The obelisk replaced an earlier market cross, and Aislabie bore more than half the cost, as well as providing the limestone from his own quarries at Studley. Designed by the celebrated Nicholas Hawksmoor, it has been shown to be the oldest freestanding monumental obelisk in the country. In 1781 John Aislabie's son, William, a Ripon MP for sixty years, had the obelisk restored in the year of his death. The plaque which an appreciative City Corporation added four years later implies that he was the original builder, to the confusion of later generations. The obelisk is 90 feet high and is topped by a rowel spur and horn, symbols of Ripon's ancient crafts and customs. Originally four small obelisks stood at the corners of its base, but these were removed in 1882. The obelisk was extensively restored in 1985.

Market Day, Ripon.

2. The Market Place has been the hub of Ripon's commercial life since the 12th century when it was laid out by the Archbishop of York as one of his new towns. It soon provided a handsome income from rents, tolls and other dues. The regular weekly market, seen here in about 1907, is a reminder of the fairs and markets that have been held on the Square for centuries. One such was the Cattle Mart, which was transferred elsewhere in 1898 after strong complaints about the filthy condition in which the cobbles were left. Two years later the Square was concreted over to provide a cleaner and more level surface. The omnibus in the foreground of the picture was used to convey passengers to and from the railway station, which lay on the northern outskirts of the town.

3. The visual impact of the Square stems from its size and spaciousness, especially when reached down narrow streets. Until late Victorian times the approaches were even narrower, and in the north-east corner a block of property halved the width of what is now Queen Street. When street widening began, the owner of the business facing on to the Square held out for appropriate compensation and the case went to arbitration in 1905. The owner (Rayner) was awarded £4,827, and the Corporation had to pay all costs (£1,200). The widening of Queen Street brought an end to the practice of siting some market stalls in front of the shops along the east side of the Square, as seen here.

4. A busy market day scene looking towards the Cathedral, just before the First World War. Croft and Blackburn's Motor Works (later Morrisons) had opened on the Square, but cars were still something of a rarity.

Market Place, Ripon

5. Another market day of about the same date. Beyond the motor bus can be seen the Cabmen's Shelter, provided in 1911 for the benefit of local cabdrivers by Miss Sarah Carter, daughter of a former mayor. In later years it fell into disuse, but in 1985 Ripon Civic Society undertook the restoration of the shelter in view of its rarity value. Beyond is the Town Hall, dominating the southern side of the Square.

Market Place and Cathedral Towers, Ripon.

6. In 1801 the Town Hall was newly built 'after a design by Mr. Wyatt of London, at the expense of Mrs. Allanson of Studley, comprising Assembly Rooms, a Committee Room for public meetings and for business of magistrates'. Benjamin Newton, Rector of nearby Wath, 1816-1818, mentions going to Ripon Assembly a number of times in his diary. In 1859 a clock was added, given by the Horticultural Society during the visit to the Yorkshire Agricultural Show. Below the clock, the text from psalm 127 'Except ye Lord keep ye City ye Wakeman Waketh in vain' was added in 1886 during the great festival of that year. The Corporation made increasing use of the building during the 19th century, and in Queen Victoria's Diamond Jubilee Year (1897) the whole building was presented to the city by the Marquis of Ripon. Notice the Post Office housed in the building next door, which later became the Lawrence Ballroom. The date is about the turn of the century.

7. One of the few remaining mediaeval timber-framed buildings in Ripon, the Wakeman's House was once the home of Hugh Ripley, the last Wakeman and first Mayor of Ripon (1604). The house was once part of a much larger double-winged hall house which lay at right-angles to the street and was entered down a passageway. At some stage, perhaps about 1600, the parlour wing was refronted and made to face on to the Square by the addition of oriel windows. In 1918, with much of the original house destroyed, a room was added at the rear as a wartime Food Kitchen but was never used. In 1938-39 the Corporation was keen to have the building pulled down, but fortunately it was bought by a local philanthropist and survived. It is now used as the Tourist Information Office, and has a small Local History Museum at the back.

8. The Sergeant-at-Mace precedes the Mayor in civic processions, carrying two of the city's treasures – the 17th century Great Mace, and a baldric studded with the badges of Wakemen and Mayors from the 16th century to 1886. From the baldric is hung the ancient Charter Horn, reputedly received by royal grant in 886. The horn is bound in silver, and the horn bands carry emblems of former trade guilds. Originally under the terms of James I's charter of 1604 there were two Sergeants, to attend the Court of Record and to make proclamations and arrests. One of their tasks was to ensure that all tradesmen had been admitted Freemen by paying the appropriate fine to the Corporation. One Sergeant, Thomas Dinsdale, who died in 1874, had held the post for fifty years; together with his father and grandfather, the family had held office for 117 years.

The Ripon Hornblower

9. According to ancient custom, the Wakemen had to 'cause a horn to be blown every night during the time he is in office at nine of the clock in the evening at the four corners of the cross in the Market Stead and immediately after to begin his watch' (1598). The watch continued until dawn, and during that time the Wakeman was responsible for law and order in the town. A rate was levied for this service on every house, but victims of burglary had to be compensated. Ripon still has its hornblower, and the horn is blown nightly at nine o'clock at the four corners of the obelisk and afterwards outside the home of the Mayor. It is claimed that this ceremony has never lapsed, but the time of blowing has been altered in war-time to suit the coming of dusk. The horn seen in the picture was acquired by the City in 1865 and is still in use today.

10. The Thursday market is officially if belatedly opened at 11 am by the Bellman, who interrupts the proceedings by ringing his bell to announce that trading may begin. The ceremony appears to have developed from the time when the Bellman opened the Corn Market. The Corporation then had the right to levy a corn toll known as the 'Market Sweepings'. The Corn Market no longer exists, but the opening ceremony has survived to become one of Ripon's 'ancient charms'.

11. The Studley Royal Hotel in the Market Square, as it was perhaps in the 1920's. Renamed the Studley Royal in the 1870's, when the Marquis of Ripon was becoming a figure of national importance, it was previously known as Proctor's Hotel, and even earlier as the Norfolk Arms. Note the carriage entrance.

12. Tom Crudd, also called Thomas Spence, but best known as 'Old Boots', was an inn servant at the Unicorn Hotel, one of Ripon's coaching inns and for many years the city's premier hostelry. During the turnpike era, stage coaches for Leeds, London and Newcastle changed horses at the Unicorn, as too did scores of private carriages. Passengers were often entertained by 'Old Boots' who, as well as offering boot-jack and slippers, would hold a coin (which he kept) between nose and chin, for their amusement and his enrichment.

13. Despite being labelled 'Westgate', this view is of Kirkgate, about the time of the First World War, but later than 1916 when the Palladium cinema opened. The cinema helped to provide entertainment for the thousands of soldiers based at Ripon during those years. Narrow, winding Kirkgate is the ancient thoroughfare between Market Place and Minster Church, and as such is the route still followed by civic processions today. Modern Kirkgate is choked with traffic, but otherwise differs little in general character from Edwardian times.

SERGT MESS "D" BATTERY. R.F.A.
RIPON. 1917.

14. A scene from Ripon Camp in 1917. Work on constructing the Camp began immediately after the outbreak of war and it was eventually to house some 80,000 soldiers over a huge area on the western and southern outskirts of the city. It formed a complete township with its own roads, lighting and even branch railway. This postcard was presumably made available to the public after 1918 since military photographs were not permitted during the war for security reasons. A business man from Edinburgh even found himself brought before the magistrates for taking a photograph of the Cathedral, and was sternly rebuked.

15. The Northumberland Fusiliers, no doubt on manoeuvres, in camp at Ripon in 1907. The site is Redbank, where the racecourse had been situated from 1865 to 1900 and the former grandstand building can be seen in the background – now the Cathedral Choir School. The use of this area for army training seems to have been well-established before the Camp of 1914-1918 was built. Even by then, Ripon had a long history of accommodating the military. In 1810 the Corporation resolved to complain to the Secretary of War 'respecting the oppression of the Innkeepers and inhabitants of this Borough by having soldiers quartered upon them so long' – in this case the 15th Regiment of Foot.

16. A delightful picture of an Edwardian Whit-walk by Sunday School parties in their best attire, proudly bearing their banners down Kirkgate to the Cathedral. The date is thought to be 8 June 1908. A newspaper account of 1904 described how *children bring flowers and other gifts which are afterwards distributed amongst the sick, poor and children's hospitals. Sunday School banners are carried and the walk is by way of Allhallowgate, Finkle Street and Queen Street, thence via the Market Place to Kirkgate and the Cathedral. The gifts of flowers, etc., are collected at the west doors of the Cathedral.* In 1904 550 scholars and teachers took part from the Cathedral and Bondgate Sunday Schools, 15 from Jepson's Hospital and 30 from the Girls' Home. The Co-operative Stores can be seen in the background, soon to be moved to new premises in Park Street.

17. Winding Kirkgate suddenly offers a fine view of the Cathedral, framed by buildings on either side of the road, as artists have appreciated since the days of Turner. Here the setting is typically Edwardian.

18. Kirkgate again, crowded with people caught from the photographer's window as they stream back from the Cathedral towards the Market Place in their best finery. The occasion is unknown, but the groups of children with their banners suggest that again it may be Whitsuntide.

19. The entrance to Westgate as seen from outside the Town Hall, in days when pedestrians had little to fear from traffic. The Freeman, Hardy & Willis building with its interesting cupola, and the Bank at the top of High Skellgate, were both built about the turn of the century. The cupola survived as late as the 1960's, but regretably is now gone. The widening of Westgate had begun, as this picture shows, and although never finished, in its next phase was to claim the two pubs seen on the right — the Queen Alexandra and the Green Dragon.

20. Fishergate at the turn of the century, looking towards the Market Place. Although still narrow today, its width was doubled in Edwardian times. That meant demolition (about 1906) for the Grapes Inn, at the corner of Lavender Alley, but only after protracted legal delays over the licence. The inn sign (a bunch of grapes) still survives in the Ripon Museum collection. Across the road can be seen the antiques shop of W. Hemsworth, collector of local bygones and Mayor of Ripon from 1922 to 1925.

21. Known for centuries as Horsefair, this relatively wide avenue running north from the Market Place was renamed North Street in the 19th century. On the left can be seen Winsor's fish, game and poultry shop, and further along, St. Wilfrid's Hotel, both now gone. Smithson the butcher, however, on the right (marked 'Our House') still flourishes, one of Ripon's oldest established businesses.

22. During the 19th century the Post Office occupied four different sites in the town centre: originally it was on the Fishergate corner of the Square, in a building later reduced by road widening; then in 1859 it was moved to Kirkgate; a few years later it was on the east side of the Town Hall, and then on the west side (as seen on No. 6). The smell from a slaughter house at the rear may have encouraged the next move, to a site in North Street adjoining Kearsley's Engineering Works. The new Sorting Office that was built there (1905) can be seen in this picture. This too has now closed, and the present Post Office is in Finkle Street nearer, once again, to the Square.

The Clock Tower, Ripon.

23. North Road, leaving Ripon. The Clock Tower, the subject of the postcard, is barely distinguishable in the distance. Much more prominent is the Congregationalist Church, built in 1870 to replace an earlier chapel for Independents (1818) off Allhallowgate, now marked only by its graveyard. The Congregationalist Church has gone too, as elsewhere the victim of changing fashions in religion, and in its last years suffering the ignominy of serving as the warehouse of a poultry firm. A block of flats now occupies the site. In Victorian times North Road bore constant traffic between the Railway Station and the town centre. Lime trees, given by the Marquis of Ripon, were planted in 1880 to provide a pleasant approach to the city and ornate rows of fashionable terrace houses grew up along the route.

24. Sited at the junction of North Road and Palace Road the Clock Tower was erected in 1897 to commemorate Queen Victoria's Diamond Jubilee, and it appropriately incorporates a statue of the Queen herself. The Clock Tower was the gift of the Misses Cross of Coney Garths. The Tower was also intended no doubt to add further enhancement to the appearance of North Road.

G 7760 RIPON MINSTER, WEST FRONT.

25. The much admired West Front of the Cathedral was built in the early 13th century by Walter de Grey, Archbishop of York, and is in the Early English style, characterised by rows of tall, slim, pointed, 'lancet' windows, arranged in groups. Victorian restoration work re-emphasised the simplicity of the early English style by removing later additions. The two west towers had timber spires until they were removed for safety reasons in 1664. The pinnacles on the corners were added in 1797, but have now also been removed (1940).

26. The Cathedral viewed from a vantage point in the town, across a jumble of pantile roofs and tall chimney stacks. In the Middle Ages the palace of the Archbishop of York stood hereabouts.

Ripon Cathedral from South-East

27. A view of the cathedral from a popular angle, probably taken in the 1920's. The East End was built on sloping ground, which contributed to its collapse less than half a century after the late Norman church was completed. When rebuilt (about 1300) it was strengthened by a cluster of buttresses, but the south-east corner has had to be underpinned in modern times owing to continuing structural problems. Most of the gravestones in the foreground have now been laid flat.

28. The great geometrical east window, reglazed in 1854, dominating the chancel is seen here in Edwardian times. In later years the oak pulpit (1862) near the window was to be removed and the altar furnished with a new reredos commemorating the local men who died in the First World War. The canopies of the choir stalls are largely the work of William Bromflet and the famous Ripon School of Carvers; they were made between 1489 and 1494.

29. Dignitaries leave the Cathedral to face the choir, a Guard of Honour and a throng of onlookers. The Mayor can be seen, next to the Sergeant-at-Mace, but it is thought that hidden from view may be a royal visitor, perhaps the Prince of Wales, or Princess Henry of Battenberg, both of whom are known to have visited Ripon in 1905. This excellent photograph also shows how important hats were in those days.

30. Consecrated Bishop of Ripon at the age of 43 in Westminster Abbey on 25 July 1884 by the Archbishop of York and seven other bishops, the Right Reverend William Boyd Carpenter had previously been chaplain to Queen Victoria herself, and was much esteemed by her. Renowned as an able speaker, he was also the author of several theological works. He served the diocese for 28 years.

THE PALACE, RIPON.

31. A spacious stone building designed in the Tudor style by William Railton, a London architect, the Bishop's Palace was built 1838-1841, and occupied by the then Bishop of Ripon, the Right Reverend Charles Longley. Longley was the first bishop of the newly created diocese (1836); a former headmaster of Harrow, he was later to hold the archbishoprics both of York (1860-62) and Canterbury (1862-68). The Palace stands about a mile north-west of the city on the road to Masham. In 1940 it was superseded as the episcopal residence by the more modest Bishop Mount, and later underwent conversion to a Doctor Barnado's School, still its use today.

Bishop's Palace, Ripon   Valentines Series

32. Another view of the Palace, showing the bishop's private chapel added in 1848. The east window of the chapel is a memorial to the father of Charles Dodgson (Lewis Carroll), a canon of Ripon Cathedral and Archdeacon of Richmond. Lewis Carroll is thought by some to have derived inspiration for some of his fanciful literary characters from misericord carvings in the Cathedral, whilst on visits to Ripon.

33. This fine limestone building was constructed early in the 17th century as the residence of the Dean, an office established by Royal Charter in 1604 to head the Chapter of Canons. Considerably altered in the 18th and 19th centuries, it ceased to be the Deanery in the inter-war years and is now a restaurant. The main internal feature of interest is a massive oak staircase in the hall. In the 15th century, the Bedern College of Vicars-Choral stood on this site, replacing an even earlier Bedern on Bedern Bank.

34. In Edwardian times, as this picture shows, the west side of Bedern Bank was lined with an assortment of properties, ending with the King's Arms public house at the foot of the hill. A misguided scheme of the 1930's for incorporating Bedern Bank into the line of a new inner relief road (past the Cathedral!) led to the progressive demolition of these properties well into the 1960's. Then suddenly, an entirely different route for the new road was chosen – but by then the King's Arms, one of Ripon's oldest hostelries, was long gone (1959).

35. The clearance of Bedern Bank led to the destruction of neighbouring courts and yards, including York Yard, seen here. Although the clustered roofs provide an attractive foreground to this view of the Cathedral, such yards in Victorian times had frequently been crowded and insanitary slums.

36. Thorpe Prebend House faces the Skell, not the Cathedral, but its origins lay with the church. During the Middle Ages, one of the seven Minster canons had his residence here; he was supported by the income (prebend) from the nearby village of Littlethorpe — hence the name Thorpe Prebend. But canons were often absent and prebendal houses fell into disrepair; in 1391-92 we find Thorpe Prebend House used as a workshop for the casting of bells. The Reformation led to the secularization of much church property and about 1609 Thorpe Prebend House was rebuilt as a gentleman's town house by a wealthy York merchant, George Dawson. In April 1617 James I stayed overnight in Ripon on a journey northward and is reputed to have enjoyed Dawson's hospitality here. The wall-creeper and stocks have now gone, but the interesting roof of mixed slates and pantiles remains.

37. The house contains a fine 17th century staircase and early wall panelling. The windows, however, have been much altered and when the house was restored in 1913-14 it had to be converted back from five cottages. It was given to the city at that time by Miss Darnborough, in memory of her brother, for use as a museum but this function was surprisingly allowed to lapse in 1957 and the museum collection largely dispersed. Thorpe Prebend House is now used by local community organisations but is badly in need of major restoration.

38. Near Thorpe Prebend is St. Annes, another large house of considerable age with gardens running down to the river. At the time that this picture was taken (1920's ?) St. Annes was serving as a residential annexe for Skellfield School (see No. 40).

39. Next to St. Annes (seen on the right here) is St. Agnes Lodge, which makes a fine contribution to the houses of historic interest and architectural merit in this street (St. Agnesgate). St. Agnes Lodge is a 17th century building with much early timber work, including roof beams, panelling and staircase. The cluster of circular windows is most unusual and was perhaps inspired by the Norman Chapter House windows visible from here. Out of sight at the end is a huge chimney stack, and on the riverside front a fine Dutch gable of about 1690.

40. The dormitory of Skellfield School — one of several private schools set up in the town in the 19th century. Founded in 1877 it occupied Alma House by the Skell footbridge for the next fifty years, and then in 1927 moved to Baldersby Park, later to close there. The school laid strong emphasis on individual development and won itself a high reputation locally.

Magdaline Chapel, Ripon.

41. The hospital of St. Mary Magdalene lies on the northern outskirts of Ripon, close to North Bridge. It was founded by Archbishop Thurstan in the 12th century as a house for religious sisters and given a particular responsibility for caring for blind priests and lepers. The Leper Chapel remains intact, with Norman south doorway, stone altar slab and Perpendicular east window. Victorian additions — a second chapel (1868) and two blocks of almshouses — can be seen in this picture, taken at the turn of the century.

Holy Trinity Church, Ripon

42. On the west side of the town stands Holy Trinity Church, whose tall broach spire has been one of Ripon's most prominent landmarks since it was built in 1826-27. This cruciform church, in the Early English style, was paid for by the Reverend Edward Kilvington out of funds provided by the bequest of a relative, Thomas Kilvington, a local doctor of note. The church could seat 1,000, of which 200 places were to be 'free' in accordance with the foundation terms. It quickly became the Tradesmen's church, as opposed to the Cathedral, which was for the upper class. The Grammar School held their commemoration service there until 1930. In 1984-85 Holy Trinity Crypt was restored and refurbished for parish use.

The Catholic Church, Ripon.

43. A fine building designed by Joseph Hansom and built in 1862 in the Lombardo Early Decorated style, this church is unusual both in style and plan, with the tower surmounting the apsidal sanctuary. Together with the priest's residence and school, it cost £5,000, a large part of which was provided by Fr. Philip Vavasour of Hazlewood Castle, his friends and his family. The new church replaced a meeting room in Heath's Court, Low Skellgate, used from the time that Roman Catholics were permitted public worship after the Reformation. In 1888 the window above the high altar was erected in memory of Canon Vavasour. Other windows and many furnishings came later from the private chapel at Studley Royal.

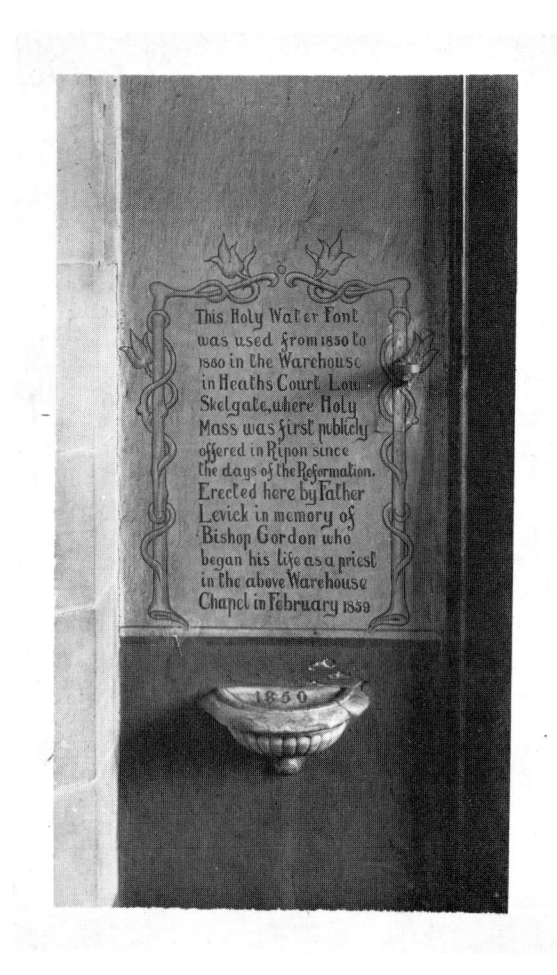

44. The Holy Water Stoup brought from Heath's Court.

45. The Feast of St. Wilfrid, Ripon's patron saint, is first recorded in the 12th century, when it took the form of a fair of four days in April. In early Victorian times an effigy of the saint was brought into the city annually, to commemorate his return from exile, but by the Edwardian period a real 'St. Wilfrid' was making his way through the streets, preceded by the City Band. In this picture the street is Kirkgate.

46. Another glimpse of the saint in Edwardian times. Since 1962 the occasion has developed into a procession of carnival floats, which ends appropriately at the Cathedral. As the picture shows, the appeal to youngsters has always been strong.

47. Ripon acquired a taste for festivals in 1886, when it held the great Millenary Festival to commemorate its 1000th anniversary. Other festivals followed in rapid succession, and in 1904 the opportunity was taken to celebrate the 300th anniversary of King James I's Charter of 1604. The pageant 'King James and the Wakeman of Ripon in Merrie Old Days', seen here, was produced at the base of Ailcy Hill, a huge mound near to the Cathedral. No stage was needed, as nature provided the scenery and set.

48. Another scene from the 1904 festival. That same year the foundation stone of the new Spa Baths was laid (see No. 52) and the theme of this float is 'Queen of the Spa', with maids-in-waiting.

49. Yet another festival was held in 1906, over three days (July 19-21), to celebrate the 20th anniversary of the Millenary Festival! Here St. Wilfrid and a throng of stern attendants prepare for their part in the inevitable pageant.

50. The draycart of Hepworth's Brewery, fully decked out for a festival occasion, possibly the 1935 Silver Jubilee. The brewery was in Bondgate, by the iron bridge. The business had earlier belonged to the Lumley family, but in the 1880's direction passed to Thomas Hepworth. He died in 1892, aged 51, but the business flourished long after his death. Years later it was to be absorbed by Vaux Breweries of Sunderland. The prevalence of horses and other animals in the town over the centuries gave rise to problems of cleanliness. In 1633 the Mayor gave notice to all householders that they were 'to sweep before their houses and not suffer any rubbish, dunghills or the like to be in the streets, which is a thing commonly practised to the great disgrace and prejudice of the town and corporation'. Modern litter problems pale by comparison.

Aldfield Spa. (Source of Ripon Sulphur Water.)

51. In Edwardian times Ripon tried hard to emulate nearby Harrogate and develop into a fashionable spa, conscious no doubt of the economic benefits that would accrue. Enthusiasm was not diminished by the fact that the nearest medicinal waters were at Aldfield, over three miles to the west, and a special pipe line was laid to bring them into town.

52. In 1905 the new Spa Baths in Park Street were opened, the brickwork finished in yellow terracotta. To the right of the carriage porch can be seen the entrance to the Spa Gardens, with the Spa Hotel in the distance beyond. Immersion baths and the latest electrical treatment were available, in addition to glasses of sulphur water, to treat a variety of ailments including asthma and gout. The Marquis of Ripon expressed pleasure with the appearance of the buildings and grounds, but when asked to drink the water begged to decline, remarking that the smell was quite strong enough to knock him down.

53. The ornate interior of the Pump Room, finished with tile, marble and stained glass. The Baths were open from 7 am to 7 pm, the admission charge was 1d, as too was a glass of sulphur water. As elsewhere, the spa declined in the inter-war years and in 1936 a public swimming bath was incorporated into the building, reflecting new tastes and habits. Even today, however, sauna is available and much of the original character of the building was restored at considerable cost in the early 1980's. Refurbishment of the foundation stone (1904) unexpectedly revealed a cache of newspapers, documents and coins of that date.

54. The Spa Baths were formally opened on 24 October 1905 by Princess Henry of Battenberg, the widowed youngest daughter of Queen Victoria, and her daughter Victoria Eugenie, who was to become Queen of Spain the following year. The spectators and Guard of Honour await the arrival of the royal party, on its way, no doubt from Studley Royal.

55. The Guard of Honour comes to attention as the royal carriage arrives.

Spa Gardens.   Ripon.

56. Adjoining the Baths, the Spa Gardens afforded visitors the chance to relax, chat, get fresh air, or just listen to the band. The fine wrought iron bandstand was erected in 1903. The Sunday concerts in the Spa Gardens generated fierce controversy in the local press (1905). The Mayor's objection — that people were being paid to work on Sunday — was applauded, but the band played on.

Spa Gardens, Ripon

57. The Spa generated a demand for accommodation and the result was the Spa Hydro (now Spa Hotel), built in 1906 next to the Gardens by Sir Christopher Furness of Grantley Hall on the old Elmcroft estate. It opened in 1909. In the foreground is a statue of the Marquis of Ripon (see no. 59) a great local benefactor who died that same year. The statue was unveiled on 4 May 1912.

58. The billiard room at the Spa Hydro in its early days.

59. The Marquis of Ripon (1827-1909) was a public servant of national importance. Born at 10 Downing Street, whilst his father was briefly Prime Minister, he went on to pursue a distinguished career with the Liberal Party, supporting progressive causes and holding many high offices in government. Nevertheless he still found time to become Mayor of Ripon (1895-1896) and took much interest in local affairs, especially education. A replica of his statue was erected in Calcutta, a reminder that he was once a distinguished Viceroy of India (1880-1884). A convert to Roman Catholicism, he was buried in the family church at Studley Royal.

THE QUEEN THANKING THE DEAN OF RIPON (DR. MANSFIELD OWEN) AFTER HER VISIT TO RIPON CATHEDRAL, AUGUST 20th, 1923.

Reproduced by permission of the "Yorkshire Evening Post."

60. Queen Mary visits the Cathedral on 20 August 1923. She was staying at Goldsborough Hall with Princess Mary (later the Princess Royal and a Freeman of Ripon). During the conducted tour the party viewed the new reredos (see no. 28) and the Caxtons in the Library. Queen Mary is known to have been a patron of Hemsworth's antique shop, but on this occasion she was on her way to lunch with the second Marquis of Ripon at Studley Royal, reputed to be one of the finest game shots in the country. Only a month later he was to die suddenly on the grouse moors.

The College, Ripon from Hockey Ground.

61. Built in 1862 to train women teachers for Church of England elementary schools, the College is seen here some 40 years later in Edwardian times, little changed. Subsequently, however, it was to undergo major expansion as well as alterations in organisation and purpose; it is now a mixed College of Higher Education on two campuses (Ripon and York) and is no longer exclusively concerned with teacher training.

62. On the left is the early chapel, and on the right the science wing. The central block, built in 1904 and enlarged in 1912, was demolished in 1930 after severe subsidence problems. The hockey field in the foreground is now occupied by tennis courts and a car park.

63. The staff Common Room at the turn of the century, furnished very much in the style of the times.

64. Ripon's Grammar School is of mediaeval origin and stood for centuries in High Saint Agnesgate, near the Collegiate Church. The church connection, however, resulted in its closure (1547) during the Reformation, but only a few years later the school was re-established and re-endowed (1555). Three centuries later, the need for more room compelled a move to the outskirts of the city, and land was generously provided by the Marquis of Ripon at Bishopton Close (1874). A boys' school until merging with the Girls' High School in 1962, Ripon Grammar School has produced many distinguished scholars and churchmen, and has adapted well to the demands of modern society.

Ripon Cathedral, from Banks of Skell.

65. A delightful view of the Skell, seen here early in the Edwardian period, making its way to Ripon through verdant countryside. Abundant tree growth in more recent years now unfortunately inhibits much of this vista. (For the Rustic Bridge, see no. 66.)

66. The Rustic Bridge lies close to the point where Skell and Laver meet, and permits those enjoying the riverside walk in this area to vary their route. A romantic and attractive bridge as first constructed, it was later spoilt by insensitive repairs using wire mesh; in 1984, however, the superstructure was rebuilt appropriately in timber by Manpower Services Commission workers, who also carried out other improvements to this local beauty spot.

67. Bishopton Bridge carries the main road west from Ripon across the river Laver towards Fountains Abbey and Pateley Bridge and, not surprisingly, a bridge is recorded here from mediaeval times. In the 14th and 15th centuries it bore the chapel of St. Mary, and in Henry VIII's reign an unwelcome hermit had to be removed from it. The bridge was much widened and improved in 1884-85.

68. Perhaps the 'Esegel' Bridge mentioned in mediaeval times, Borrage Bridge is referred to as such from the 17th century. It now carries A61 traffic south from Ripon, but in much earlier times gave townsfolk access across the Skell to Borrage Green, common land where the burgesses had the right to graze their cattle and horses. In 1765 it was rebuilt, a move linked perhaps to the rise of Harrogate and the turnpiking of main roads, but even in 1865 it could be described as 'narrow and incommodious', and today, despite modern improvements, it is quite unsuited to the size and volume of traffic which it has to bear. The downstream side of this picturesque bridge is of grey limestone, while the upstream side has been widened in sandstone.

69. Further down the Skell, Bondgate Green Bridge has carried the eastbound traffic out of Ripon since the closing years of the Napoleonic War. It replaced a narrow footbridge which stood a few yards downstream, and its stone-flagged foundations can still be seen when the river is low. No doubt the greater volume of traffic in the Coaching Era compelled the construction of an adequate road bridge here.

70. Yet further down the Skell is Alma footbridge, first built in 1862 through the efforts of Thomas Stubbs, former Governor of the House of Correction, who lived nearby in retirement. Battered by winter floods, the bridge has been much repaired and renewed over the years, but as seen here, in about 1900, might well have incorporated some of Stubbs' original structure. In this classic view of the cathedral, Alma Weir can be glimpsed through the bridge rails, with tannery buildings beyond. In the 19th century the weir fed a mill-race, but with the demise of the mill (1939), the weir became a neglected crumbling eyesore. Happily, in 1984-85, a new weir (for measuring the flow of water) replaced the old, and the river banks were restored and landscaped.

71. Only a short distance below Alma Bridge is Woodbridge, a similar footbridge of no great age. It stands, however, next to a ford still much used by local traffic and probably of great antiquity.

Ripon, from the Railway Station.

72. This view of Ripon was enjoyed by visitors leaving the railway station early this century. The railway connection had begun in 1848 with the construction of the Leeds-Thirsk line and was to last until the drastic economies of the 1960's. New arrivals who spurned the omnibus service to walk into town came at once to North Bridge across the Ure, a structure of enormous length designed to span the entire flood plain of the river. The bridge is first recorded in the early 13th century, and by the 15th century bore the chapel of St. Sitha. Money from the offertory box and from bequests went towards maintenance, but still in 1608 the bridge was 'in great decai', and in 1821 floodwater damage nearly claimed the stagecoach 'Telegraph' at night. Local pressure led to the bridge being doubled in width in 1880-81 at a cost of £7,000, of which £1,500 was raised in the city.

Boats on the Ure, Ripon

73. Boating was a popular Edwardian pastime in Ripon as elsewhere, and the river Ure offered excellent facilities – although heavy rain in the Dales could bring sudden danger and there were many fatalities over the years. In the distance can be seen North Bridge and beyond it the railway viaduct (now gone). The building in the top corner is the Pumping Station which provided the city's water supply from 1865 to 1888; recurrent flooding problems finally compelled the authorities to seek an alternative source elsewhere. Bathing, as well as boating, was a popular diversion, and a bathing pavilion was later to be built here by Dr. Freemantle, a former Dean.

74. One of the most attractive of the Dales rivers, the Ure passes close by Ripon on its north and east sides and for many years formed the boundary between the North and West Ridings. Though not nowadays known as a salmon river, in 1486 it was necessary to issue an order that 'no one shall catch in the waters of the Yore any salmon called salmon fry, sive les kepers'. (Kepers were salmon which had spawned.) Calm and refreshing in a hot summer, the waters often surge angrily in winter and recurrent floods over the years have brought much destruction to property and livestock. In 1869 a major disaster occurred at nearby Newby Hall when a ferryboat capsized, drowning nine horses and six members of the York and Ainsty Hunt, including the Master, Sir Charles Slingsby, in the swollen river.

Hewick Bridge, Ripon

75. Hewick Bridge, near the Racecourse, carries the road to Boroughbridge and York across the Ure. Like North Bridge it is of mediaeval origin, and also bore a chapel – in this case dedicated to St. Anthony. In 1478 we learn that there was 10½d in the offertory box. Celia Fiennes, visiting the area in the 1690's, described the bridge as 'pretty large, with several arches... often out of repair by reason of the force of ye water that swells after great raines; yet I see they made works of wood on purpose to breake the violence of ye streame; and ye middle arch is very large and high'. A comparison with the picture shows what major rebuilding proved necessary over the next 200 years!

CIVITAS RIPONENSIS

RIPON.

HERALDIC SERIES

76.